The Cubist and the Lost Notebooks of the Painter's Wife

"Self Portrait"
19" x 23" circa 1972
Jennifer Glancy Brouillette
"In my painting / my eyes were cherries. / My mouth a small wedge of cherry pie in a background of orange and red"—section 2, *The Lost Notebooks of the Painter's Wife*

The Cubist and the Lost Notebooks
of the Painter's Wife

DIANE GLANCY

RESOURCE *Publications* · Eugene, Oregon

THE CUBIST AND THE LOST NOTEBOOKS OF THE PAINTER'S WIFE

Resource Publications
An Imprint of Wipf and Stock Publishers
199 W. 8th Ave., Suite 3
Eugene, OR 97401

www.wipfandstock.com

PAPERBACK ISBN: 979-8-3852-5430-9
HARDCOVER ISBN: 979-8-3852-5431-6
EBOOK ISBN: 979-8-3852-5432-3

VERSION NUMBER 07/10/25

Who is tending this sun, this moon?
Who moves them around?
There must be somebody to look after this world.

—A Nisenan prayer

CONTENTS

PORTRAIT FIGURE AT THE MET

British Columbia, ca. 1840
Wood and pigment

The Charles and Valerie Diker Collection of Native American Art

The Haida woman represented in this carved figure wears a pleated cotton dress and holds what appears to be a
wafer in the mid-nineteenth century. Haida men and women made regular journeys to Victoria,
British Columbia, five hundred miles
south of their homeland on Haida Gwaii, also known as the Queen Charlotte Islands.
The woman likely acquired her garment there, and the wafer
may refer to the Christian Eucharist, perhaps symbolizing
her religious conversion.

The new ones took her animal skins
and put her in a cotton dress that made her shiver.
Her hair parted and greased to stay in place not blowing across her face
as she worked. As she walked to church. The eucharist stickum also.
Large, flat and round in her hand.
Each bite made smaller.
At night the moon nearly gone.
It was the old priest who ate it.
And the Spirit made him spit it back into the sky.
Its steel hands pushing his stomach until it came out.
The old priest held the plate under her chin so crumbs would not fall.
The rodents would come. The dogs would howl.

She would wake at night and crawl with vermin.
Maybe it was the old priest who poured the crumbs into the sky
when he wandered there at night looking for his God.
Alone on the reservation his thoughts got past the birds
with their beaks that pecked the windows.
They would throw their bodies against the glass
while at vespers. The moon waning and getting bigger.
The old priest's mouth moved like a beak.
His eyes turned into black stones.
His black hairs were feathers on his arms.
It was said at night he flew with Christ who tried to run away.
To make a clean sweep.
To escape the hoosegow the new ones brought.
How it happened long ago. The mystery of being.
She could feel the ice-bit fingers of Christ on her toes.

1.

Perhaps they will come again next year—Chief Winnemucca [after seeing white men]
Life Among the Piutes, Notebooks of Sarah Winnemucca, 1844–1891, reproduced from the 1883 original,
Sierra Media, Bishop, California, 1969

I took the last of his paintings to the art dealer in Reno. I had given the dealer my notebooks of the
painter's words to draw attention to his work. I hoped they would be published, but somehow they were
misplaced. The dealer didn't know where. Maybe in the storeroom.

If you could have seen the place, you would know why they were never found. I was furious. What would I
do now? Recreate what I could of the painter's words? And how would I live?

You know where they are, the dealer said, driving me from his store after another visit. Yes, I knew—they
were in my head.

I tried to write what I could remember of the words I heard the painter say. But the colors shifted.

Blue is not the sky. Not the sea. But the edge of a road as it disappears over a hill. Blue is alone. By itself.
Blue is the edge of sleep. Blue is a slope over which I fall each night and face the dark so unknown I cannot
wake.

BELT CUP AT THE MET

Great Lakes, Canada or United States, ca. 1820
Carved wood and metal nails

On loan from the Charles and Valerie Diker Collection

*In the three-dimensional narrative on this expertly carved wooden cup, a school
of lake sturgeon watches over an industrious beaver colony. Nineteenth-century Anishinaabe representations
of water-related animals referenced communal songs and stories, with themes of sustenance, abundance and
protection. Shining eyes on each animal, created with tiny metal
nails activate their presence. The enclosed handle made for easy transport when worn
on a belt or carrying strap.*

Galloping they galloped
galloping galloping horses and cows.
The land itself could hurry the cattle.
The heels of his boots worn down.
Glove lost.
He cut his hand on barbed-wire.
A pulled hangnail already red.
Galloping galloping. His jaw tightened.
He couldn't yell the herd away.
They had the instruments of their cries.
His mouth wouldn't open to drink from the turtle-shell cup he took from an Indian.
The metal nails of its eyes piercing his hand.

I left the painter's ashes in the dry bed of Winnemucca Lake, as he asked. I drove there alone, wanting no one with me. I sat on the rocks. Beside the ancient petroglyphs. I visited the places we had gone together— now evaporated in the hot, barren air.

In my painting
my eyes were cherries.
My mouth a small wedge of cherry pie in a background of orange and red.

At one time I painted [before I saw Lloyd was the painter].

What was the origin of orange?
Red and yellow certainly.
I remember thinking that orange was an animal.

The air sometimes was orange when wildfires burned in the hills.

There were welts in the road in the desert.
Little rises where wind had blown the dust in rows as if sorting.

If I guessed, I would say the orange fragments of rust we found
were pieces of the earth when it first formed as iron.

DEAREST PSALMIST

Thou art my rifle. The beasts dwell around me. In the forest
they grumble. I think they will come forth. Dear Psalmist,
thou art acquainted with the abundance of beasts. They
wear apparitions on their heads. I see them in the dark.
They growl. They are old as earth. You are my shield. My
bucket. My roundtable. My Holy Hill. Psalmist.
Conqueror. Chief. You are righteousness. You are grief.

3.

I never minded the long trips from Winnemucca to Reno with Lloyd's paintings.[1] I thought of them as children I was driving to school. The land passed slower the farther away it was. If I listened hard enough, I thought I could hear it speak. I felt sometimes as a child, I would be swallowed by its enormity. If the land spoke, it had a mouth. If it had a mouth, it had teeth.

Often I was on the road when the spirits struck. They made little whizz sounds. Sometimes a cluck on the windshield if they threw pebbles from their landing wheels. They looked sloppy. You'd think they'd dress not in work clothes.

For a vision, I saw two plaids that didn't go together. As if a plaid painting in a plaid frame. Two voices in tandem. Distant yet connected.

I stand in the yard watching the tattered edge of clouds cross the mountains. I take the laundry from the line, fold it in the basket. In the dust, I see prints of the mountain lion that visits our yard at night. Maybe I am the mountain lion that sleeps beside the painter at night.

1. 125 miles west on I-80, Nevada

THE BATTLE OF YELLOW HOUSE CANYON

March 18, 1877

Destroy thou them O God—Psalm 5:10

Because the rocks looked like yellow houses the Span-
iards said *Casas Amarillas*. Because they drove stakes
into the High Plains to find their way across the table-
land they said *Llano Estacado*. Because Medicine Lodge
Treaty gave Comanche and Apache hunting grounds
Black Horse slaughtered an American buffalo hunter
picking off buffalo until his ammunition ran out. Be-
cause the buffalo hunter was found with his stomach
cut open the American buffalo hunters took revenge.
Because it was nearing the end of the Buffalo Hunters'
War Black Horse raided the hide camp with Apache
and Comanche. Because it was a battle of the Buffalo
Hunters' War the Spaniards were not there to name.

4.

Lloyd
Lightning moves like a piece of furniture across the sky.
Not a bolt of lightning, but a sudden flare of light in the distant clouds solid as a chest of drawers.
I see the shapes of clouds in the lightning.
They are ghost shapes for my paintings—

[Segment]
The critics said his paintings were plain as wallpaper.
Simple as house paint.
But he kept painting in blocks of yellow, pink, blue, red.

Lloyd
Last night, the full round moon was a hay-roll over the mowed field.
A moon so bright I could hear my wife—
who left the ceiling light on up there?
Now I wanted yellow for the moon.
I wanted to smear the canvas with nothing but yellow
as it turned the corner on a bicycle.

When the last of the buffalo on the Southern Plains were killed. The wind lifted dust from the land as if the whole earth were migrating. There was a crack of dry thunder in the distance as if buckshot. Then the terrible silence.

5.

You should keep a journal, I told the painter. But he wouldn't write down any of his ideas. You see, these journals of his are mine. I took the notes I heard him say, but neglected to write.

I listened when he talked to himself—or talked to the paintings. I listened, but never heard them talk back—though I think he heard them.

I held my wooden spoon in the batter, stirring and stirring as I listened to his words. They couldn't be left in the bowl. Unbaked. A color takes shape according to the ideas it creates.

THE CUBIST

Thou has smitten the cheekbone.
Thou hast broken teeth—Psalm 3:7

O Lord the feet are running. Large as a hay wagon.
The sheep in the field are balls of onions. Their round
bodies abide. He must be in another house. The horses
chase the road. Between the trees the clouds ousted in the
sky. Lord skewed and triumphant. The stalks are cut. The
stubble hard to cross. On the blue house a white door. The sheep
clumsy if there is delay.

6.

The spirits kept shipping boxes. I could not make them stop. Boxes of words. Untamed. Irreconcilable. At times, I tried to get away from them. Taking the interstate through the desert. The random back-roads.

The boxes still showed up.

Lloyd
What was I trying to get at? Assemblage from a different point-of-view? Theory in the narrative set?

A world made of two disconnected forces—the object of the particles—the relativity of the abstract. Working a thin line of gravity between them.

A small transport. Something like a postage stamp.

RACHEL PLUMMER'S NARRATIVE OF TWENTY ONE MONTHS SERVITUDE AS A PRISONER AMONG THE COMMANCHEE INDIANS

May 1838 Indians raided the Texas settlement.

They took Rachel and her son.

She never saw him again.

She was expecting another child.

She became a slave to the Comanche.

The Indians killed the baby when it was born.

It was interfering with her work.

Rachel was ransomed by Mexican traders.

Returned to her husband.

Rachel bore a third child and died shortly after.

The child died two days later.

7.

Footnote [2]
I woke with a dream. I was a child standing on the floorboard of the back seat. Looking at the passing land. The land flat and passing. The brush moving with us in the distance at a slower pace. The land just coming out of winter. The trees without leaves. What makes sense in a dream? I was in a different land. A place I had traveled as a child. The memory tucked away like a kerchief in a drawer. I was moving over the land. The moving more than the staying. The house where we were going. Someone in it. My grandparents in Winnemucca, probably. Though it didn't matter. Only the moving to get there. The smell of wood smoke on the air. The dusty road. Some sort of desperation. Dryness as a form of parole. Look at them. Anointed with plainness. Nothing reaching another. This is a car. This is where it will take you. A bowl of land. A cloth of linseed oil.

IMPOSSIBLE INVASION FROM THE NORTH POLE

Because the world is shaped as an onion is shaped.
Because looking down from the top
it was assumed the whole ball was white.
The frozen sea.
The peaks of ice.
The endless slabs of snow.
If they had known
the whole world was not white
they would have abandoned their sleds that were difficult
across the desert
to cross.

8.

My grandmother had a necklace of bright wooden beads—large beads—blood red. I put them in my mouth. She didn't like it and slapped me to make me let go. I howled, of course.

Red is awake now. It is walking toward me.

I tell Lloyd's colors to be quiet. Sometimes they don't like to be beside one another. I hear them fuss. I tell them, a single color is not interesting until another color is added to it. Then dialogue starts between the colors.
I could hear them say, move over. You're in my way. Quit crowding me. Find somewhere else to go. I don't want to stand next to you.

Eventually one of his paintings sold.
I pay cell phone. Utilities. I go to the grocer's. Milk. Milk. At the art supply in Reno I buy a tube of paint without letting it slip into my bag.
Eventually the art dealer in Reno wanted more and more of his work.

Eventually Lloyd taught his craft.

He painted an Indian with a disgruntled face. Straight nose. Square eyes. The usual feather blowing west-ward from the head. Breast-plate over a shirt with striped sleeves something like the apron I sometimes wear.

THE WORLD IS DRAWN ON WHEELS

He copied manuscripts.
A little pillow behind his back.
A blanket over his knees.
A small rug rolled under his feet.
The cold draft on the floor.
Gloves without fingers.
A distraction at first—the marginalia.
A dried leaf of the bean-vine caught in the window's edge.
The note of a bird's chirp.
What was that animal?—woodchuck?
Opossum? Squirrel? Racoon?
The field beyond the window covered with snow.
He copied their tracks in the margin of the manuscript.
The wind rattled the roof of the monastery.
The monk coughed.
The wool cowl chafed his neck.
Manuscripts day after day.
He made more notes in the margin to ease his boredom.
It was the first act of disobedience.
A departure from endless task.
The chariots of God are twenty thousand—
the monk copied Psalm 68:17—
and drew a line of wheels descending the page.

9.

Lloyd
I look at colors until I find what they say—the way lightning at night exposes the clouds hiding there.

Would you believe the yellow that is behind brown?—or the blue beneath the black? I cover the canvas with yellow paint. I let it dry. Then I wipe it off—or what I can of it off.

I begin over-painting with another color—the brown—or the blue and then the black of blue. Those solid colors are not solid. They are a passageway to the story underneath.

Yellow is a horse loose from the corral of His Greatness, the Sun. Yellow is the edge of a word. It is the memory of a field so white it is yellow. So bright I close my eyes. A brilliant spot stays on the inside of my head. A visage. A sun spot. Yellow walks behind the eyes.

Now it is evening. His Greatness has left the house with his walking stick. He is gone someplace else to stir the heat.

A WAY THROUGH THE OCEAN WITH WHEELS ON THEIR SHIPS

If I could open my jaw.
The waves high with the wind breaking against the boat. All of them winded
by wind.
The vehicle letting down the sail tossing sideways.
The boat headbutted by water as it made long ruts in the waves.
The first road was a wagon to the shore. A stagecoach to the ocean.
An avenue to the withered place of docks
and shipyards that were going to carry onward across the water to land
not knowing where they went. Or what monsters of the deep.
And when they arrived
there was another voyage across another land.
The bears and wrens. The hornets and grouses. The voyagers in their
trousers and loose blouses
where villages established their houses. They stayed for tractor-pulls and
molasses.

10. MUKAT AND TEMAYAWIT

Mukat and Temayawit appeared. From there they went outside the door. They went where it was bare, where there were no relatives. Mukat made people. Temayawit made those who dwell[2] in the distance—At first the sky was a heavy sheet of metal. Holes had to be poked. The sun was a saw-blade. It lived behind the brush, coming up from where it spent the night. The windows were punch-out cards to let in light. Temayawit made the umbrella. He made the moon. He made night-goggles. He made flood-lights. The people Temayawit made were far away. How to reach them from where they went. Mukat called into the distance—hello—hello—but could not hear them. Sometimes Mukat saw lines between the stars. He made telephone poles to reach the people—but poles fell down in snow, and could not always go as far as people went. Mukat tapped his head with a magic rock and thought of semiconductors of charged particles that turned the voice into sound waves and sent them to masts across the land he also made. But sometimes the voice went everywhere. Temayawit saw stars gathered in their constellations. He made a grid-work for the places where people were. It directed Mukat's voice to them—and theirs to his. Mukat went out in the cold to feed the horses. Temayawit broke the ice in the trough for the cattle. Tumbleweed rolling on the ground. Geese honking with their arms held out to the air.

2. Beginning fragments from a Cupeño creation story, "Water We Believed Could Never Belong to Anyone," Karr, Steven M., *American Indian Quarterly*, Summer 2000, Vol. 24, Issue 3, p 381, after which the piece departs on its own.

WAHPENA'S KITCHEN

A kitchen tamed the wilderness.
A stick on the tongue to taste the cooked meat of the buffalo.
The first stove was a brush fire.
Prairie fire.
Open campfire.
Rub sticks / make fire was the first command.
An arsenal.
Arson.
Devil's work.
With his forked tail.
He could skew.
He could use his hot temper.
Roasting turtles in the oven.
Roots.
Seeds.
Pemmican.
Devil's food.
A fire is listed as tactile.
The flint.
The sulfur.
The flames.
Its fingers giving themselves to the air.
On the menu—
squash
bison burgers

blueberry sausage
blue corn topped with huckleberries
venison meatballs with blueberry sauce
homemade chili.
In the beginning fire was riddance.
Not used to make provision.
Leviticus 10:2—there went out fire from the Lord.
Revelation 20:9—and fire came down and devoured them.
Genesis 19:24—fire and brimstone
charcoal and burning ash.
Numbers 11:1—the fire of the Lord burnt among them.
Even to the uttermost parts of the camp.
Who said kitchen work was easy?
Long hours.
Regulations.
The monks, priests, robed women, whoever came
with their orders one after another.
These things you shall not eat.
Food with the memory of trauma.
Displacement of Plains Indian tribes.
Kickapoo.
Sac and Fox.
Others.
Each has the mark of the forbidden.
She watches them as she beats her stir-spoon against the bowl.
At one time she would have licked.
These animals are unclean to you.
Leviticus 11: 4–6—
the camel, the coney and the hare chew the cud but divide not the hoof.
The swine divides the hoof but chews not the cud.
What rules the new ones brought.
The unclean animals she cooketh in the kitchen she hath made clean.

11.

I let his words dry. Wiped some of them away. I used his process to keep his journals. It's what the painter called, under-painting.

It was Indian faces he drew in shapes of green and ghostly white—He made teeth like a picket fence. I said he was a cubist, disrupting structures to reassemble them, which he did with color. Buckets of it.

How can he use his lovely colors on those distorted figures? They all are back-lit or lit from within—as if there is a hole in their skin where an odd light burns. At first, I didn't want to sleep in the same house with them.

A mountain lion comes down from the hills at night. I hear it in the yard. I think it waits outside our window. I hear it pant.

Footnote [55]
Sometimes an idea starts with a fragment—*I felt in myself something going.* What did that mean? Was my driving an attempt to break away from something I didn't know? Was my driving an attempt to get back to what was?—what would have been in place that was fundamental to my being? Transposed. Transmogrified. Outlawed. Made fugitive. That road coming and going at the same time—always a part of the trip. A note on the process of journey. In travel ideas form. I have to be moving. The same as the brush over the canvas until words cover the page.

I made biscuits in triangles, folding them over. I had an old pair of scissors. They squeaked like birds when I cut. Once in a while, the painter looked up from his coffee.

Color is sacred—I heard him say. Burnt ochre. Umber. India red. Pipestone. Persian Gulf red. Carbon black. Cerulean blue. Chinese white. Dutch white. Flake white. Mars yellow. Iron yellow. Nickel azo yellow. Munich lake blue. Sap green.

After breakfast, the painter went to his studio. I wished I had something to absorb me. Work—that's what he had. I sat at the kitchen table with my head in my hands. It was then I began to hear the voice of colors. White is a stove. It is a canvas passing from the cold of a desert night to the heat of mid-day.

THE SPACE THAT WAS LEFT HAS BEEN A SOURCE

Instead of this, I tell
what I hope will pass as truth—
"The Loneliness of the Military Historian"
Margaret Atwood

part one

I shared my room with a brother. Possibly a chest of drawers. A toy box with a lid
that fell with a bang. There were no longer bears or wolves. But there were dangers. There was nothing when
I asked the walls what there was to do.
The ceiling was silent also. It was all it was.
The vacant lot down the street. A bird dived at me once as I got close to the nest
it built in the thicket that seemed to call me into it. I told the bird.

part two

At one time Indian scouts looked for soldiers and wagon-trains that would come
and come. When it was thought the first ones were stamped out—they had taken on
the lives of those that came. They hid the old ways with twigs and locust-wings
and stones wrapped in a kerchief.
The settlers continued with wagons and wagons until there was no room.
They removed the wheels and stacked the wagons one on another.
The wheels kept moving. Tongues and axels from piles of wagons were comets
they had to duck.

12.

Footnote [fragment of] [8]

Lloyd
Yellow has a temperature. It is the color of His Greatness, the Sun.

I make something there, the painter said to me. I make something there also, I answered. I make corn-bread out of nothing. I borrow flour and lard. I have a cup of sugar and an egg. This is my art—I make cornbread that crumbles because I have only one egg. The painter thought about the egg. He wanted to paint a horse the color of a yolk. I shared the cornbread with the neighbor where I borrowed the lard and flour.

I visited a gallery with the painter. The frames were more interesting than the paintings—made of fabric that didn't match—plaids, stripes, floral as my kitchen curtains, solids, spots—the fabric stitched together with wide white threads.

That night I would walk in the yard but the mountain lion was waiting.

To Establish the Truth and Healing commission on Indian Boarding School Policies
in the United States and for Other Purposes.[3]

He dreamed of a giant with a very small head—a crow's head.
His black wings a cape.

He slept with fleas, varmints, ticks and other vermin,
toothache, arm that healed crooked in a splint his mother made of sticks.

At night, the howl of wolves, coyotes.

He dreamed of his tribe wandering the plains, hunting small game and buffalo. crossing creeks, setting up
camp.
Now the crows in black capes built boarding schools for children.

Now he slept in a large room with beds and cries of children, and footsteps to silence them.

If he didn't look to the man raised into the air on a stick, he would be in hell.
They have no rest day or night.
The smoke of their torment goes up forever.[4]

3. The main purposes are to understand generational trauma, and to find children buried in marked and unmarked graves and
return the bones to their tribes.

4. Revelation 14:11

If not terror enough on open prairie—blizzard, rainstorm, windstorm when cottonwoods hissed and tepees ballooned, heat storm, stillness when no leaf stirred, drought when animals fled—

Now the horrors came from the pages of their Bible. Brimstone and fire burning hotter than summer prairie heat.

The lessons in the classroom. The crow before him. The hard bench. Table where he laid his hands to be hit.

13.

The threads on the fabrics were sutures, actually, holding the differences together.

In the gallery, he got the idea to paint the suppurated Indian. The chronic Indian. He used violet and black with a stark white face-mask marked with the sutures he saw in the gallery. The Indian as his horse. The horse as the Indian who rode. The two becoming one.

I say painting is truth. I say it is lie.

A train is a scar across the desert.

A painting is an abstract of construction. A mountain lion rumbling in its throat. Listen to the little cog wheels turning as it hunts. Maybe it waits by the window for the spirits to toss it a few rodents.

Later in the day, I visit the farmer's market. Pears, apples, melons, radishes, pomegranates, cabbages. Slicing through them, later, to integrate, to interpret them, I cut my finger. It is blood that tastes like color.

No. It is color that tastes like blood.

BOOK OF NAMES OF THOSE WHO DID NOT RETURN

Kuper Island Residential School—
Mona, Samson Harris, Thomas Mason, Alfred McKay, May Nysok, Lucy
Gordon, Sophia Edgar, Samson Edgar, Eva George, George L. Humchitt,
Reggie Allen, Molly Irene Moon, Andrea Helen Alfred, Douglas Benson,
Jackie Archie James, Anderson Sye, Clara Andrew, Adolph Maurus, Lawrence Thompson, Joseph Ignace, James Louis George, Stanley Joseph,
Andrew Tom, Cecil Williams, Alice George, George Johnson, Jessie Lucas, Catherine Marshall, Rose Johnson, Moses Tom, Agnes Amos, Lorena
Thomas, Mary Vincent, Samson Mclean, Joan Manson, George Quisot,
William Maquina, Dora Noshkepy, Arthur, Tillian Mckay, Edward Arnold, May Harris, Bella Peter, Katie Manulth, Sophia Noothlena, Carrie
George, Simon Tom, Emil Howard, Frank Ubaldus, Cosmos Ya-Epoutle,
Felix Antoine, Eline Frenchie, Amanda Frenchie, Caroline Jacob, Catherine Jacob, Samuel Anghame, Simon Gontek, Francis Johnny, August
Tseleokanum, August Jimmy, Modest Kosteinagant, Samuel Whonock,
Theophane Johnny, Josephine Jacob, Ellen Moses, Jules Tseleskampten,
George Baptist, Josephine Norris, Yinnito Taylor, Jack Williams, Taylor Santo, Mary Taylor, Maud Jackson, Katie Taylor, Bertha Fred, Mary
Bob, Violet McKay, Dalton Silver, Norman Bob, Lily Pearl Smith, Edward Thompson, Virginia Moses, Cyril Mussel, Maisie Shaw, Ramona
Taylor, Herb Robert Green, Gary Ross, Shirley Leslie Williams, Mary
Elaine George, Mitchell Joseph, Gerald Wilson, David Thomas, Gary
Hapkins, Gary James Hopkins, Ivan Wilson, Nellie Kiutesi, Annie Jack—

I wrote the stage for you. The floor. The curtains. I wrote for you a set. Table and chairs. An ottoman. The windows of the house were open. You moved with your swift hand. Shutters blew across the yard. The wind transported cows and horses half a mile. The barn as if a gum eraser passed over it. I wrote for you transitions. The church was left half standing. The steeple hanged like a broken mast. Boards were found a mile to the north. In the churchyard the dead stayed in their storm shelters. What wild band-music of weather. What game event. The blowing away of everything. The clearing of the deck. I left a book of literary techniques for you. Segment. Fragment. Truncate. Decollate. I gave you stage-directions. The characters moved from one end to the other. I described the theme for you. I gave you plot. You glued one star back onto the sky. The quarter moon was left tilted. I gave you the subtext. From that you could deduct the text. Water is hardest to handle on stage. It is the highest form of art.

BOARDING SCHOOL

Dem peoples dat go away to dem schools
an come back you know dey really suffer.
Stories of the Road Allowance People
Marie Campbell

We ate a man in the wafer
the monks and priests put in our mouth.
Chew. Swallow. They said.
Drink his blood.
They had to be mean as the world to Him was mean.
He was stricken on the cross because of us.
We didn't remember doing.

15. NORTHERN NEVADA COLLEGE

Sometimes I hear the fragments of his voice.

Lloyd
Can you pick up another tube of umber?

Hallah
We owe him money. I took the last tube of paint you asked me to get.
I think he saw me.

Lloyd
They have asked me to teach at Northern Nevada College in Elko.

Hallah
They called you?

Lloyd
I applied. They called and I drove there for an interview.

Hallah
When?

Lloyd
Last month. You thought I was in the desert painting.

Hallah

You didn't tell me?

Lloyd
We'll have income.

Hallah
Your work brings income?

Lloyd
Don't make it harder than it is.

They traveled in five wagons from Wounded Knee.
One with hay and oats.
Another wagon—rations of coffee, bacon, flour,
beans, hard tack.
The other wagons carried prisoners, soldiers
and a sullen Indian agent.
They camped in gullies, ravines and brush
along a slight ridge beside the trail.
The massacre backhanded the air.
The wind was by their side.
They heard a cry for water but did not stop.
Birds flew above them.
The wagons followed a line thinned by shadows.
Blue Hair, Round Moon, Wood Pile were silent.
What could they say after the desolation of the tribe?
What survived when light was killed?

16. THE MOVE [1]

I pack the kitchen.

A new colleague from Northern Nevada College in Elko brings his truck. We load our table and chairs. Our bed. My canvas and paint. Evalee, an old friend, and a friend of hers help.

I put my mother's dishes in the trunk of the car. I hug Evalee. Lloyd gets in the truck with the colleague to drive 100 miles east on Interstate 80 from Winnemucca to Elko.

We leave the house vacant in case we want to return. The neighbors will look after it. We leave the roads Lloyd and I drove into the desert. The church stays behind with its high steeple. A rafter over Winnemucca to hang on. Or was it Golgatha? My grandmother would not be happy that I didn't know the Bible. She used to test me when I was a child.

We are on our way to a job. Lloyd and his paint. The bread of his wife.

I follow Lloyd and his colleague. Lloyd had two paintings that were not dry enough to move. I told him I could come back for them, but he didn't want to leave them behind. He stayed up late pounding boards, making a rack for them in the backseat of the car.

We climb Golconda Pass. The land is brown. The mountains. The valleys between them. We pass Iron Point. At Valmy, there's a rest area. I call Lloyd on my cell and tell him I have to stop.

Already?

I'm nervous.

They drive ahead when I stop. They are slower and I can catch them.

I make note of the signs I pass—Battle Mountain. Mote. Near Dumphy, on the plain land, I see a red truck with cargo wrapped in green, blue, white. I thought Lloyd would be looking, but I see him talking to his new colleague.

Then a cobalt truck with cargo wrapped in navy tarp.
Trains are color in the desert too.

I watch the basins between mountains. It seems like the land had been pushed together.

I watch the side of the road—The scrub brush is russet—There is the thorny ground cover my grandmother called, goathead. My grandfather called, puncturevine.

I remembered names. Camel thorn. Stonecrop. Knapweed. Malta star-thistle.

Mostly, there is the pale gray-green sage with its yellow blossoms. The round bushes are baby heads along the road.

I feel the land is hardly moving.

Near Elko is Button Point. Emigrant Pass [altitude 6114].

Maybe it will be all right. The brown mountains look like loaves of baked bread. Their ridges—the crust.

The pillars on the mountains west of Elko stand like the ancestors.

We arrive at our small place and unload.[5]

5. The next day Evalee calls. I left on the back porch-light. The house is locked. Unscrew the lightbulb, I tell her.

Forgive our mistreatment of the Cavalry. Of the settlers in their wagons crossing the land where
we hunt. We thought they were animals covered in white hide.
Forgive our raids. Our burnings. Our murders. Forgive our inattention to the monks & priests who came to
torch our lives with His. Christ of the incoming.
Of the misdirected. To promote our adoration through pain.
We didn't get in step as they thought.
They crowded us with reservation and boarding school.
Later in the morning
when a helicopter crossed the sky
the boughs cut off were at our feet.

17.

In the desert there is momentum.
A train with several engines—a line of rail-cars for them to pull.
What would the train do with the power beyond what it is called to do?
Those are the early years for the painter.
An engine forward. An engine backward joined together.
Sometimes a train waits on a side-track while another train approaches and passes.
A train is a moving canvas.
See the graffiti and primitive figures painted on the rail-cars.

ON THE SEA THERE IS NO SHADE

By noon the sky has turned to cream.
The fish are rocking back and forth.
The sea has large, round eyes as if a basin or large bowl.
I write a letter on the oar.
I push the letter out to float.
The sea is wide and dark.
By night, the stars are kicking in the sky.
The heavens have a search light for a moon.

18.

I read him   the newspaper   a tornado wiped the   pasture of a horse-
farm.   Most dead. One found   alive   on roof of   crumpled
school. He only hears   horse   in air legs fly   pasture split
cormorant   [that inserted from where?]   You   listening? I ask.
What? He looks   and nothing   he   makes   sees.[6]

Lloyd painted a face nearly purple as the shadows he saw in the mountains. He left the face featureless because of the erasure Indians have known.

The profile of an Indian against a black background—say, the middle of the night. Above him, the edge of a pull-down shade with the ring on a string hanging from it. The ring on the window shade is the Indian with a hole in the center. That's what he wanted to paint. He had to find the Indian traveling toward the canvas. He heard the steps. Muffled.

He had to get the Indian away from how they have been seen. To see beyond how they are seen.

The Indian wears a horror mask for a face. Feathers radiate from his head as if a child's drawing of the sun with its rays sticking out.

6.   In the silence that followed the tornado—the sound of gunshot as wounded horses were put down.

HE HAS A TRAILER FULL OF TIRES JUST SITTING IN THE YARD

Plague Mask [1650–750]
Deutches Historisches Museum, Berlin
This authentic plague-doctor mask is a recognizable symbol of Black Death

The first plague was a tiger in Africa
A deer on the Atlantic
A lemur from China
A polar bear in the Arctic
Witches fell from the sky
And built fires
The people sacrificed their lives
A plague-doctor mask had a bird-like beak
Stuffed with herbs, dried flowers, spices
The proboscis [what is the plural of proboscis]
[Before Pinocchio]
The people held rituals with bat faces
But a small voice said smaller, smaller
Smaller still—
So small no one could see what transmitted to another
The plague-cause was something they could not see
The doctor covered his face and head to ward off the bite
From whatever it was that bit
He took animal-skin and made a cap
That covered head and face
And a long nose to filter the air he breathed

The people made rattles
They shook trees
Watched firebrands as they went out in the air
The woodcarver Geppetto carved a puppet of wood
A marionette actually that moved on strings
The first plague caught them unaware
Killed 75 million 1346–1353
Then the next and the next
The 1918–19 flu epidemic killed 50 million
Covid-19 [2020–] to date 5 million
The plague-doctor wore a bird mask with red glass eyes
A wide-brimmed hat
Black overcoat
Breeches as if waders for the nearest trout stream
A Medieval hazmat suit
A wooden cane to direct without touching sick patients
Death was in the wind that blew
A flea bite
Or could enter through the nose and mouth and eyes
The sun that appeared and left
Taking with it the light
Leaving another night where dreams entered
The nose, the eyes, the head
In village, woods and forest
The doctor made an animal-hide head-piece
A mask over his face and head
A sea-diver's helmet
With bulging eye-holes covered with glass
Whatever plague [pandemic]
A trailer full of tires
Against locust, cricket, mosquito
Whose bite caused death
To be sure it is a tale of bravado

To walk into the sick rooms of moaning victims of the plague

Whatever form

A sickness that is backroad poverty

Old ringer washers

Broken-down cars in the yard

Engine parts

Carpenter's rusted tools

Blowtorch

Memorabilia, relics of travel

A pilgrimage to a Canterbury to pray to God

Who brought strife

The irritant Pinocchio

A pupplet

Until a fox and cat bound Pinocchio's arms

And put a noose around his neck and hanged him from an oak tree

Until we know the origin of the sickness that comes

Until we stand

On a couplet of the soundest ground.

19.

—its cells have burst, its tissues have been torn—
Francis Ponge, from L'Orange, 1942[7]

Once I fell from a train when it stopped in Reno. I tripped on the steps. I was two. I was wrapped in a sheet while my nose and upper lip were sewn up.

To this day, I don't like anyone close to my face.

A train is a body wrapped in a sheet. Arms held flat to the side against the body. A train with the stitches of its crossties.

7. Francis Ponge, 1899–1988, a French essayist and poet influenced by surrealism. Ponge also developed a form of prose poem minutely detailing everyday objects. Wikipedia

SNOW FENCE

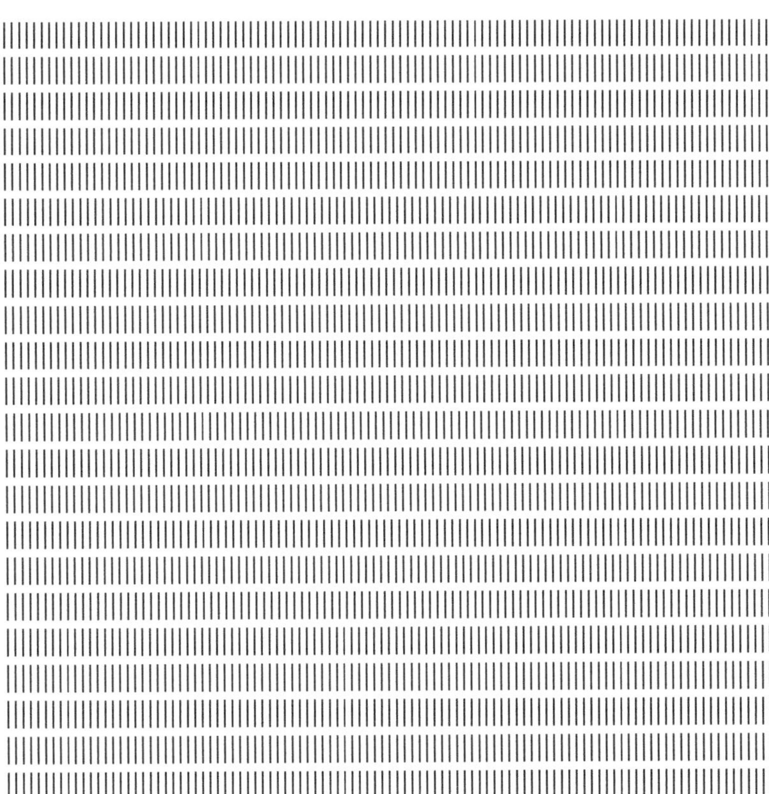

20.

What exactly is Indian art? [This from Lloyd.] A portrait of the noble savage? The drunkard on the street? It's hard to look at the decimation of a people—but it's in America's past. The country must remember on some level even if we've squashed it inside the national memory—and think it isn't there. Put your hand in the air—you feel it fly—

A recurring dream starts before I sleep. I see black and white ghost faces haunting the air. Their faces line the ceiling. They sit along the top of the walls. Their teeth are pieces of the moon quartered and diced—chopped by my wife on her cutting board. Their noses flare when they smell a brush fire. Or maybe it's the cooking fires at the mission. They look for the land as it was before the mission cramped it. They are wild with memory. Their anger looms. They fight the walking stick of His Greatness—Chop. Chop. Their mouths open in a snarl. Sharp teeth bite.

I paint the torments I see in the faces of Indians. I paint the faces when they are blinded by rage. Dulled with alcohol. A washed-out past washes over them.

I am Indian. I am not Indian—as Fritz Scholder said.[8] If I am not Indian, what is this that roams through my head?

8. Luiseno painter [1937–2005]

THE LORD ON HIS FJORD

Where are you when I call to you, my Lord?
Are you wrapped in rabbit-skin in your chair?
Is it in your Book your promises stored?

If my cold fingers played a guitar cord—
If the arctic fox danced with the white hare—
Where are you when I call to you, my Lord?

Are you still reading while the blizzard roared?
And Northern Lights moved with a frantic prayer—
Is it in your Book your promises stored?

If my cold feet walked on a diving board—
If ice is surf board to the polar bear—
Where are you when I call to you, my Lord?

The ocean is shifting and I am not shored—
If I built an igloo not round but square—
Is it in your Book your promises stored?

I am on loose gravel and you are moored.
When cold winds howl and the world is a snare—
Where are you when I call to you, my Lord?
Is it in your Book your promises stored?

21.

I attended a workshop with the non-narrative poet who taught the online class. I read my narrative poem and received comments from the workshop.

After I read the piece, _________told me to take out everything but—say—9 words—

Part One

The Man Who Loves Dreamsicles

He reads the wrapper with rapture—
Let the Dreamsicle warm a moment before eating
so it will not stick to the tongue.

He unwraps the Dreamsicle watching the crystals form as it warms.
He studies the striations of frost on the orange coat of his Dreamsicle
as the earth's atmosphere touches it.
Maybe he is like Christ walking through the wheat field
or Van Gogh studying sunflowers.

The man who loves Dreamsicles is delighted as figures
in Piero di Cosimo's *The Discovery of Honey* [1498],
an early form of the Dreamsicle.

He is passionate as El Greco's *Adoration of the Magi*
[1565–67] in orange Dreamsicle hues.

Or his *View of Toledo* [1596–1600],
in which Dreamsicle flames burn at the stake
during the Spanish Inquisition.

The man who loves orange Dreamsicles has red hair and beard.
He is Van Gogh's *Self-portrait Eating a Dreamsicle* [1889]
or his peasant family, *The Dreamsicle Eaters* [1885]
in a dingy room in Holland.

He is held by the oranges in Pieter Bruegel's [the Elder]
Peasant Wedding [1656].
Or Paul Gauguin's *The Vision after the Sermon* [1888]
in which an angel wrestles with Jacob—
the angel's wings white as the inside of a Dreamsicle.
Or the splash of Wassily Kandinsky's
Sketch for a Composition VII [1913]
as we move toward the modern Dreamsicle.

There's also Paul Klee's *Twittering Machine* [1922]
where birds made with line and dot
tweet the song of an ice-cream truck circling neighborhoods
in summer.

Jackson Pollock could abstract Dreamsicles too.

I think also of Christofino Allori's
Judith Holding the Head of Holofernes [1613].
Her bodice orange as a Dreamsicle.
[Holofernes was about to destroy Judith's village of Bethulia
when she went into his tent with her saber and removed his head.]

In 1905, 11-year old Frank Epperson left a glass of soda
on the porch on a cold night in San Francisco.

The next morning, he found it frozen, and pulled the soda from the glass
with the stir-stick he had left in the glass.

In 1923, Frank Epperson introduced the Popsicle to a crowd
on Neptune Beach in Belmar, New Jersey.
Then came the Creamsicle.
Then the Dreamsicle.

The man who loves Dreamsicles has visions of paradise
where Dreamsicles float in the air redolent as orange blossoms.
He sees radiance in the Dreamsicle orange
of Rosso Fiorentino's *The Descent from the Cross* [1521].

I actually saw a picture of Martin Luther King, Junior
giving his *Ihaveadream* speech in Washington, D.C.
with a Dreamsicle photoshopped in his raised hand.

Maybe George Washington ate a Dreamsicle when crossing the Delaware.

I think of Mars as a Dreamsicle—or the orange storm-clouds on Jupiter
voluptuous as Joseph Wright's *Vesuvius from Portici* [1774–76].

Spiral galaxies twirl through the traveling Hubble.
Their orange coating covered with a slight hoarfrost—
their inside white as iced milk pure as lily of the valley
or a polar bear.
I suppose it's the reverse of the molten ball of earth
that had to cool so grass would grow and cows could eat
and give milk for the Dreamsicle.

Once I drove through the southwest.
The wind blew fine sheets of dirt across the highway.
That same evening, the sun went down

orange as a Dreamsicle through an atmosphere charged with dust.

At 5:00 am, I woke to a gunmetal gray-black light—
as if the horizon of earth were the rim of a black light-bulb.
It's why I sleep on the road sometimes to be near the wildness there—
and to see the first tinge of orange-dawn on darkness
as if a Dreamsicle rising without its stick.

Part Two

The Erring Need of Narrative

I
Christ
with rapture
              passionate.
        A saber—
                            his raised hand.

II
There is, in the orange, the constraint of art history and the primitive need
of its form. In a wound tearing apart, the need for meaning sticks.
I could not therefore, leave the moorings—because the plop of orange—
not the fruit but the frightful separation from the known world—
would fall to indirection.
Thus, I write the idea, and not the handling.

WE CAME TO ALASKA JULY 27, 1898

Built seven houses
and a big three-story farmhouse.
We received, according to our contract, sufficient food.
The Superintendent began selling our provisions to the Eskimos
and he put the money in his own pocket.
Finally there was hunger and many came down with scurvy.
Samuel Balto, Sami, Anvil City, Alaska,
9 September, 1899

A sum of zero
built on the sum
of diminishing horizon
the emptiness of zero
out there yet
a ceremony for harpoon
the seal came to
the answer
of zero yet.

22.

Lloyd
Color should be able to be seen on different levels—I tell my students at Northern Nevada College where I take a job teaching. It is a mountain lion that consumes me.

Now I'm looking for an idea for a particular painting—The foreground will be the red of a pomegranate or radish. The background—the royal blue of a wife's anger. In the middle—the white ghost of a soldier standing on the battlefield among the dead. His hands full of guns.

I take a chair before my class of art students.

Painting is the story of the painter—

I was born in Reno. My father and mother were assimilated Paiute. We were distanced from much of what he had been. My parents were educated. It was expected of me.

The Bureau of Indian Affairs had to send the Indians at least one of their own. I think my father was the overseer of the boarding schools.

On a field trip, we went to Winnemucca Lake. President Roosevelt had named it a refuge for migrating waterfowl. But the lake had seasonal water. Eventually it dried up, and was removed from the national registry of wildlife reserves.

The petroglyphs are still there. They stand in straight lines and swirls. They could have been the veins in the wings of waterfowl—or the veins of leaves. Now the land is military reserves, storage, and test sites. I liked the mystery of the glyphs. They were from a world that left symbols of what had been.

I met my wife, Hallah, at the University of Nevada at Reno. I knew what I wanted to do—paint. She knew what she wanted to do—be my wife—which is understandable. [The students laugh.]

We tried to live in Reno, but I couldn't make a living. We moved in with her parents in Winnemucca. It was her grandparent's house. Her parents moved over for us. Her father was sick—then her mother. Finally, we had the house to ourselves.

Get used to poverty if you want to paint.

I see their interest in my art class as I talk. I tell them to draw a narrative. A self-portrait. Find their Lake Winnemucca. It is their first assignment. It will be an assignment I use for several years at Northern Nevada College in Elko.

Hallah cooks for us all on Friday nights. Then the students want to leave. They have their own lives to go to.

MAN IN AIR

Photograph of a blanket toss, c late 1800
Alaska Polar Regions Collections & Archives
Elmer Rasmuson Library
University of Alaska Fairbanks

He is in the air
as if the photograph catches him trying to rise from earth.
The blanket made of walrus skin.
The slug of a walrus.
A sloth lumbering across the shore [easy to spear].
An old oak unmovable in the storm.
Mustached, *blunderous*, with two long tusks
[from Dutch *walvis* whale and *ros* horse
from Old Norse *hrosshvalr* a kind of whale].
The man flies to see if the clouds are blubber.
The man is Sami.
The people are hungry.
The Sami in Alaska migrated from Norway, Finland, Sweden
to teach reindeer husbandry to Alaska Natives
when seal, walrus, whale hunting depleted herds.
Old whale-horse.
Old horse from the sea.
Your hide stretched into a blanket held by others
sends a man on a springboard of flight
while the photograph catches him in air, arms outspread
as if gravity never calls us back.

23.

When the bodies of the fallen were wound in orange sheets and burned on a pyre Achilles was always elsewhere—
Zachery Mason, *The Lost Books of the Odyssey*

Footnote [34]
[This inserted]   The newspaper—
A man entered   Walmart   on Potato   Road   set   fire   to   rack of   men's   clothing.

EPISTLE FROM A MIGRATING HERON

The heron stands at the water's edge.
Its neck and head like a question mark.
The box of its body on wire legs.
It could be a construct of carboard and feathers.
Like any disciple or acolyte
it concentrates on water.
Not water
but fish moving beneath the surface of the water.
A heron stands in the shallow marshes in summer.
In winter it reads its be-spotted pages,
its notes on weather,
and the frustration of finding a fish
without a ceiling of ice over it.
A heron must endure disappointment,
insects, fireflies, while nothing happens.
It's the work of a disciple to wait
in contemplation of floating ripples.
The stiff cold wind that falls.
The stutter of hail in the reeds.
The warranty of scripture
to make inquiry with an occasional scrape, a squawk,
a cough, rasp, complaint, *rawk rawk rawk*.
To lift its wings and fly southwest
to a new water's fluent edge.

24. THE MOVE [2]

scene [ ]

Hallah
Ahhhhh!!! They told me I couldn't come back. Me! The wife of faculty!
I won't let myself be accused! Someone else took the box of rice. Search them, I yelled. They took me to
the manager's office. They have been aware of my stealing. They have watched me for months. Do I want to
see the monitor? They have a monitor? They have been watching! I am angry. ANGRY—in this low-grade
place. I didn't take the package. Someone else did. They knew I would get blamed.

Lloyd
The clerk at the campus market said it was you.

Hallah
I go before the disciplinary board at the college. I cannot return to the market. I have community service. I
am watched when I enter other stores. I am innocent!

Lloyd
You're NOT innocent. You've always taken what doesn't belong to you. You have a history of it.

Hallah
I have to have something of my own efforts.

Lloyd
Don't you know it's STEALING? When you put your hand out to take a vegetable, you put it in the cart
and take it to the counter and PAY FOR IT. I don't have tenure. They can let me go.

Hallah

I have community service at the college. In front of everyone. I am humiliated. I plant culver root on campus. The flower that grows in the backyard of the house on Melarkey Street in Winnemucca—a tall, spikey flower with a whorl of leaves. I let never watered or cared for it. Those tiny clustered flowers stuck to my clothes. Those messy plants without definition. You have NO SHAPE OR DEFINITE COLOR OR FORM.

Lloyd passes with students. His wife, the lifter of goods from the market, is in the flower beds in overalls. Now I hold a rake.

I hate thinking of him with the young women in his classes.

Lloyd

I tell the students you work for the college.

Hallah

They know why I'm there.

Now Lloyd is up for tenure. He paints wildly. He talks about his work. A folio is required—his treatise on painting. I transfer his words to his college computer. I look through the notebooks I have kept in a box. I pull out his words for the folio that is required. I type them on the computer—when I can tell his words from mine.

Footnote [ ]

What now? Back to Winnemucca? Tenure denied. What other college would take him with a kleptomaniac for a wife?

READING

Merely a mediator.
"And We Should Not Get Excited"
Yehuda Amichai

One's relationship to the shape of place
or maybe the shape of space
as it is not tied down
but has in it
a series of places
as in moving to move often.
To work.
To be.
As the geography
of a paragraph
that is in a book
is one of others
held by the binding
that defines the definite shape.
Yet the cartography
is a concept of changing terrain.
The moving narrative
is the point-that-holds
the variables that circulate.
It is momentum
that is the center post
sturdy
as a cube of equal space.

25.

He told us never to take anything—
"They hang their clothes out of doors after washing them;
but they are not thrown away, and for fear some of you might take them, I tell you about it."
Life Among the Piutes, Notebooks of Sarah Winnemucca

Now everything in disarray. The people had to get used to it. Nothing configured as it should be. A spoon had no bowl. Disarrangement was normal. The little scissors still squeaked when I made biscuits. We still shared grief and held our anger in common.

There is a time in marriage when one wants to consume the other. I could trade him for a day at the market to buy what I want. He could eat my bones. I could cut him in pieces with a hand-saw. He could bury me in the backyard under the culver root.

Footnote [ ]
What now?
Not his usual despondency—his need for solitude.

The painter at the doctor. It is tuberculosis. One of the Indian diseases.

UPDATE ON THE WAGON ROAD BEHIND THE SPOTTED HORSES

I ask about weather beyond the windshield.
I ask if the canvas is tied down.
The present wind.
The sky orange from blowing dust.
The sun falls slowly into the distant line of hills.
Am I still headed for camp?
By evening the rump of horses is specked with the galaxy.

26. OLD FIRES AMONG US

While we were in the mountains hiding, the people that my grandfather called our white brothers came along to where our winter supplies were. They set everything we had left on fire—
Life Among the Piutes, Notebooks of Sarah Winnemucca

The stages of the earth—iron, rock, mud, pigment.

His paintings were various boxes overlaid with other colors. It was after we watched the train pass—all the railcars were brown—rust brown—but then came a cornflower blue car—a bright Monet blue—and later, toward the end of the long train, a pale green car—sage or sawgrass. I heard the painter groan in his throat. Color was the prey he was after.

CADDLE

(jesus
told him; he
wouldn't believe
it)
"plato told"
e.e. cummings

Say there are birds on the sandbar in the river.
Say they will take flight.
They have taken their wings from the coat rack.
In the ditch beside the county road there is water.
In the water leaves are wet hands reaching to be lifted.
A tree is folded in a book.
Its branches like pages that can be turned down at the corner
you want to find again.

27

Lloyd
Once I made a journey to the San Luis Rey Mission in southern California. The hard mission beds.
A heavy Spanish table with a cloth with fluted edges like a postage stamp. They sent hungry dogs into the
fields to chase the animals from the crops. The chickens clucking.
Christ bleeding on the crucifix.
Birds on the steeple roof.
The clanging bell that drove them all away.

There were oaks, alder, willow, fir, redwood, pine, larch.
Brown arroyos and yellow pastures.
They clipped the ears of the cattle for branding.

At night, when it was cold, all we had for cover was a postage stamp.

There was an old Indian across the field I visited. He went on with his stories several days. There were
many versions circling back to the repetition of certain images. I took my ideas for writing from his ver-
sions. The stories he dreamed came to him in pieces or fragments broken off from the whole. He talked—
not worrying about unification between the parts. However, I could see the way my writings of Lloyd's
voice would come, one after the other. They would find the trail between them. They would be linked. I
only had to do the work—

A postage stamp has little claws around its border.

IN A SMALL TEXAS SCHOOL ONE LEARNS TO WRITE

There are words on the blackboard. A settlement is there. Then it is erased. As if the settlement had been ransacked. Burned. The blackboard now a smoky haze. Each day the board is washed until it is black again. Each day the settlement is rebuilt over the blank space. It is a mouth one could fall into. The blackboard is to be written on. Its purpose is to be marked. To hold writing that is the settlement that keeps one from being swallowed. One can learn the words and write a version of the territory. It is resistance to erasure. Sometimes there is chalk dust in the air when erasers clap. One writes these stories on the blackboard from nothing each day.

28.

I feel the breath of the mountain lion on my neck. I hear it purr. Look at my ears drawn forward to hear. Look at my ears pulled back in anger. Its paw splits my sternum. It enters my body. I feel my claws. I hear the growl from my throat. I sit up in bed. I have four legs. My bloody nightgown on the floor. I creep from the room. I step through the yard and prowl the mountains. The world is vibrating with breath. Is this what he feels when he paints?

STRADDLED

The land is ugly though small yellow wildflowers
poke between the clumps of bunch grass and fescue.
I hear your steps in the brittle field.
The barren caliche.
The dry sky.
If I would come to the door.
If I would open.

29.

I sit at the table. I write his words in my notebooks.

The voice of green is shade from the sun. One afternoon I see green has four paws. When it turns, I see it
has a tail.

Lloyd
They are coming with their voices. That steady train across the desert. If there is an afterlife, it will be a
journey through color.

[for months]   [Lloyd's sickness]   [   ]   I only
thought
loss   then   and [not]   [   ]   [   ]
there was no painting any longer   though I saw   his hand   move.

LORD WOULD YOU

I took you to my house and you did not fit
in the narrow hallway
the rooms barely wide enough for a small bed
the ceiling sat on our heads
ghosts were there that wanted most of the place
but there was room on the sofa
if you moved the papers and books and the blanket
I covered my legs with
you could find a pencil caught between the cushions
we could write
you could rest your feet
we almost could be home.

30.

I am left with his paintings. And his words about the paintings. No—they are my words about his paintings. My words stolen from his mouth—

It's actually the story of paintings more than the paintings themselves.

I'm thinking about invention—the making of work. I'm thinking of the word, invention—both verb and noun. I'm inventing an invention.

In a dream, I open my mouth. My teeth are different plaids that don't match.

In the end, I am the one who prowls. I put on my claws. My tail and ears move back and forth.

I believe in documentation. It lasts longer than the show.

QUARTER MOON

To revive the archaic
Find a surface
Upon which to mark—
"The Original Condition"
Eric Pankey

Reading Yosa Buson, 1716–1784—
The whale already taken got away: the moon alone—
translated by Hiroaki Sato.
I could see the moon as a whale swimming in the stars.
The sky wide as a sea.
In that place
there was removal of object from its known place.
I was not of them.
But from another place
had come there with my parents
and would not stay.
Those nights the kerosene lamp sat unmoving in the house.
Before the electric poles poked the earth
and carried wires that brought electricity to the place.
Just that afternoon my grandmother chopped the head off a hen.
Blood stained the stump where she worked.
The plucked feathers flowered the dirt.
It was a brutal act.
The chickens still clucking knew they would be next.

But terms shifted.
There was displacement.
The brutal somehow seemed holy.
And the holy therefore brutal.
A simple act of transfer.
The moon was a whale under the surface of the sea.
The whale was a moon breaching the dark field.

31.

They cut off their hair, and cut long gashes in their arms and legs, and they were all bleeding as if they would die with the loss of blood. This continued for several days, for this is the way we mourn for our dead—
Life Among the Piutes, Notebooks of Sarah Winnemucca

Evalee   my   friend   pulled the   knife   from   my hand
after the funeral   Lloyd gone   each   day   grief   newly
if I   ANGRY she said be   quiet he is gone what   does it do to grieve?

Footnote [34]
The air moves. The ground sinks here or rises there. An evaporated lake bed. The mountain background. All turned out from form. What turned the layers upward? Once flat against the earth.

Anomaly was the word I was looking for. The atypical. In the midst of criticism. The act of inventing.

HISTORY OF TEXAS

It was the dry wind.
The howling dust.
They covered their noses.
Pulled their kerchiefs to their eyes.
Even horses could not graze.
The cloak that I left when you come bring with you.
The books.
Especially the parchments—II Timothy 4:13.
The letters I wrote to you in drought.
Folded in saddle-bags.
Sent on the backs of pack-mules.
Messages
of all that I have left.

32.

Why the fragments of memory? The lost notebooks broken before they were lost?—

To make bearable the friction of being—to redress ligatures—the cohesiveness of fragility. The work that should be separated—spread out—disconnected—not huddled together in their caves.

I could face the bare pages. The bare lake bed. All the blankness.

My plainness aligned with the plainness of the land. There was similitude.

I had outlived those I was with.

There were petroglyphs we had visited at Lake Winnemucca. Strange diamond-shaped marks etched deeply into the rock. Flames, Lloyd said once, though everyone else considered them a mystery. There were marks of a pine tree after fire—just a line for the trunk with a few perpendicular, scraggly branches after the burn.

Lloyd wanted his ashes at Lake Winnemucca. With rain they would sink into the ground and be with the ancient ashes buried there.

Nothing at the lake bed but the quietness. Nothing—but the sound of my footsteps in the sand and gravel as I walked to the car on the shore of the empty lake.

JOHN THE REVELATOR IN A GAS MASK

from *Beaded Mask*
2015
seed beads, deer hide, ermine and ribbons on Iraqi gas mask
9 ½ x 7 ½ x 6 ½ in.
lent by the Tweed Museum
Naomi Bebo, Ho-Chunk and Menominee
one of 15 featured works in a 2022 exhibit, "Air," to protest pollution
Utah Museum of Fine Arts
Salt Lake City, Utah

The gas mask was for the smoke from burning oil fields. He tells her.
The Iraqi set their own fields on fire in defiance.
And the sun and the air were darkened by reason of the smoke—
when day was night, and night was without moon and stars.

She travels through pokeweed for the relic of an old war.
Her headlight steady.
She drives her needle through small holes in the beads.
She finds the tunnels she ties with thread.
She remembers the beaver. The badger. The wolf.
The thick lakes and forest of the north woods.
She knows distant fires spread remnants of ash on the road.
She beads the gas mask white as frost on sycamores with sparse floral pattern—
a vine and leaves.

33.

What could I do without Lloyd? I had to work somewhere. Evalee stopped coming. I couldn't let her friends stay in the house on Melarkey Street. They were overriding the place.

I worked for a man who fixes furniture. But waiting for Lloyd's voice he didn't understand I didn't come to work.

In the warehouse. I said. Later. I had work for which I was made. I could not think what it was. I didn't make note of it. An orange face with cherry eyes.

His carpenter-pencil. Orange. Flat. To keep from rolling away.

The hammer had prongs from which I lifted nails from old wood. It was the work program. A cat-claw pulls nails from old wood. He said. To sell used wood.

His hammer at one end had two fingers to hold the nail-head in its grip. To expel. As Lloyd had been.

A carpenter he was coming now. A scar on his hand. Up Melarkey Street. It was him. No one else knew.

These words I write I said were his.

JOHN THE REVELATOR IN BOOTS AND CHAPS

His cowboy hat stained with sweat.

She has holes eaten in her sweater. The uneven margin of war.
One woe passed and another came.

Give me the little book, take, eat.

And she was given two wings—Revelation 12:14. A billboard by the road.
Clothed with a house—II Corinthians 5:2.

34. AN EXPLANATION TALE

Frederic Remington, *The Grass Fire*, 1908, Carter Museum, Fort Worth

In a dream. The painter appeared as an elk. His antlers were ragged bolts of light. They started fire along the ridge line. The words in the notebooks were flames. Driven from the woods—game for hunting. I saw the elk held a cauliflower. The cauliflower was the ice-ball of a comet. The painter himself was hunted. He struck fire in the brush. I could not see for the orange flames. Burning my throat. Stinging eyes. Afterwards. Undergrowth singed. Pinecones opened. Smoke trailed upward in thin lines. New life. New growth.

JOHN THE REVELATOR IN THE DAYS OF TRIBULATION

There is a cow in the pasture. Two bulls follow her. Her calf follows also. She plods in her heavy body weighted with udders. She is clothed with a house. A village of flies camped on her back.

What relentless pursuit. Who doesn't know what it is to follow? Who doesn't know what it is to receive?

In the universe at night the comets fall. Stars eat one another. Matter is sucked into a black hole.

She walks the fence-line all day for a way out. The cracked ground. The Texas high-summer heat. He said.

35.

Fragment [ ]
A few lost pages found. The art dealer sent. The notebooks had come apart. Someone had disposed of them. As I read the pages, I could hardly tell my words from his. The shuffling of it. The holding onto what was left.

I had been thinking of the painter before I slept. Remembering the mornings we sat at the table. I must have continued to be with him. But when I woke, he had gone, and I could not catch him.

Fragment [ ]
At night I dreamed other pages—but they did not survive the waking. They only were there when I slept. What use were dreams? They had their own world with an animal that prowled at night.

A GIRL READING IN THE LIBRARY

A Pawnee girl taken by Osage—escaped from them—lived with the buffalo where I learned—they have plays for winter evenings before the stars began to tell their stories. I drank their milk because there was nothing else. In the plays, they were a ship surrounded by the sea. They tried to read as the ship's library rolled over the waves. How the ghosts of the sea were ships—they told those stories? The stars told? Yes yes. They talked to one another. I slept with the buffalo. Their breath was a cave where I hid. The buffalo grunted and snored as they slept. There was something in their plays—ships of another kind. They lifted their sails and passed through the night. Then their foot on the shore. They would drive into us. Like a prairie blizzard. Fierce and pushing. Often as a girl my deer-skin dress on backward. My moccasins on the wrong feet.

36.

National Register of Historical Places

One day after visiting the desert I drove I-80 from Lake Winnemucca down the rust-orange mountains into Reno. At the Reno Train Station where I had fallen down the steps of the train as a child I walked downstairs to see again not since a child carried through the station blood on my dress the mountain lion still on the tracks.

At times I visited the Winnemucca cemetery where my parents and grandparents were buried. Lloyd didn't want to be buried there. He thought it overblown. I walked through the large cemetery, past fenced plots with different artifacts and various objects [whirligig, a child's toy-truck [rusted]—and mementoes of the dead [one plot had a bowling pin and a framed score-card.]

JOHN THE REVELATOR IN A DUST JACKET

The voice said to him, *Write*.

He would have explored the island. Found berries to eat with the fish.
But there was not time for that.
Often he did not eat, did not want to eat, but watched the rolling visions he saw—

There were angels and beasts and elders and living creatures.
It was the beasts he noticed first. He knew their stories.
They could have said, I was hunted.
I was made to work till I fell.
I was left to suffer.
But they said, *blessing, honor, glory, power*.

He took notes on what he saw when the book was opened.
He was nothing more than a scribe.

Horses brought famine and death. Stars fell to earth. Heaven rolled up like a carpet. Every mountain moved
out of place.

The visions unfolded one from another—
Out of the smoke came locusts. The locust came like scorpions.
The scorpions came like horses. The sound of their wings were chariots running to battle.
Such a horrific book.
He finished writing and wrapped it in his cowboy duster a while to cover what he had written.

37

This is the hardest work I did—the whole round trip, from 10 o'clock June 13 up to June 15, arriving back at 5:30 P.M., having been in the saddle night and day; distance, about two hundred and twenty-three miles. *Life Among the Piutes*, Notebooks of Sarah Winnemucca

---

In desperation one of Lloyd's paintings sold. The man from Reno called.

The house in Winnemucca was mine. The bills also. The car repairs.

I kept a notebook on the table. A bug zapper. Catching any of Lloyd's words that flew through the room.

I fought my need to lift something. I felt it was what I could do. I kept writing as if I was Lloyd. I had lived with him as his wife. I listened to him. Watched him.

I sold some of my mother's dishes. The china cabinet. I sold some paint I found—tubes not used. I laid low. Took short cuts. Worked at menial jobs I couldn't keep. The thought of the reformatory flanked my need to lift what I saw in the market. I searched the attic and utility shed. I sold my grandmother's standing cross. My grandfather's violin.

I heard my inability to accomplish. To finish. To continue in meaningful gain. Gainful employment was the term they used. To work without languish. To think of driving in the desert and not coming back. How one lives on the outskirts. A single string of barbed wire to hold the animals from the road. There was a rodent in the attic. I heard at night. I wanted to think it was Lloyd. He soon would be down. I lived with the sound. Maybe it was my mother in the kitchen. The ghosts of those who died crossing the desert brushed the windows. Peck. Peck. A quartet of wind blowing dust.

I stood in the room in the dark. What is an opus? One's work. Numbered. My grandfather hated Haydn's tendencies. His flux. His departure from expected structure. He would have hated Lloyd's work. I heard his voice at the table. His fist pounded. I thought the walls of the house would fall.

I only waited for Lloyd's voice. Maybe my grandfather would ask for his violin if I listened too long. I hid in the attic because I had sold it. Until the heat made me come down and find he wasn't there.

JOHN THE REVELATOR IN THE GARAGE

Waldo's Garage & Collision Repair.
A garage is the union of gust & push broom.
The mechanics of oil rag.
Fender. Door. Bumper. Headlamp.

He was called to see the Benghal tiger. To shift gears on the old Range Rover. To shape
the edges of the road with his tire tracks. His work at Waldo's Garage & Collision held to the
straight margin of the wall. Afterwards John the Revelator drove the dust roads for events. No one wanted to
attend. On Patmos the grizzly called for its den but could not find. The whole process installed. Lord you are
my radiator. My resolute. My resolution. Your hand
smashed with a spike as you became the way you were going. The road not wide enough
for all. You were the bridge that bridged the gorge. Your space grew less crowded all
the time. The arguments pushed against the wall. Until the pistons ignite.

38.

I looked for Lloyd's ashes in the desert basin. I had marked them with a Dreamsicle stick. Alone by the shrub. The finger of the air moved.

Not since yesterday when I saw him   painting.

___

[Segment]
I do not know what   the rattle of   it   was.

___

Desert bighorn sheep. Mule deer. Coyote. Rabbit. Bobcat [mountain lion]. Horned toad. Tortoise. Kanga-roo rat. Pocket gopher. Mountain goat. Big-eared bat. Sidewinder rattlesnake—

What to do with the afternoon that opened its hissing mouth? I could turn. But if I moved. It twisted anyway.

___

My arm   blue   Lloyd   painting
I forgot   darkness.   It wouldn't   speak.

I think   lockjaw.
What words   in   their   places.   From where they did   not belong.

Perhaps they will come back. Sarah Winnemucca—writing at the desk. Nevada Women's History Project. I worked on—until Lloyd said.

My ears swelled. I felt them with my swollen hand.
I had to   climb.   Fragment [part section   of]

ACKNOWLEDGMENTS

The Cubist

Abandoned Mine for "Straddled" and "Lord Would You"

Broad Wings, Long Legs: A Rookery of Heron Poems, Jim Rogers, editor, North Star Press, St. Cloud, Minnesota, for "Epistle from a Migrating Heron"

F(r)iction in conjunction with *Yellow Medicine River* for "John the Revelator in a Gas Mask"

H.O.M.E. Anthology on Antidote of Creative Expression, Michael Guinn, editor, for "Update on the Wagon Road Behind the Spotted Horses"

Imagined Theatres, 2023, Daniel Sack, editor, for "The Battle of Yellow House Canyon," "Waiting," "The Cubist" "Rachel Plummer's Narrative of "Servitude" and the Gloss—

I am taken with shape at the moment. The momentum of shape. Possibly abstract. Surreal—The arrow of inquiry. The boxing of argument that leads to entrapment. A room with four walls, floor, ceiling and equal space between them. A stage is a room actually.

The cubist script of misshapen pieces asks, how could the form of dialogue / monologue on the page translate unseen into action?—with the standard conflict / crisis / resolution? How could the audience realize the shape of language as relationships evolve?

How could history be presented as something that is still here? Recently the Oglala Sioux tribe blocked Christian missionaries from the Pine Ridge Reservation in South Dakota for preaching Jesus while excluding Lakota beliefs. The past appears as disembodied snippets in a field plowed for other crops. As if pokeweed. Though they rescinded several days later, August 1, 2022, and it was announced the Christian groups could come, but had to register with the tribe.

On the plains there is land and sky a tree-line along the creek. There in the distance—a house—cubed. Recently I bought an ice cube tray that was in the shape of a cube with sections for the changing form of water from fluid to frozen. Water also can be transformed into the shape of boiling, which must happen on stage at a high point in the drama. What other possibilities? The exploration of shapes that words make. The interruption of words that should follow unbroken in a sentence. The enjambment of the subject on one line separated from its verb on the next line with other contexts that pull it away from its object. The same disruptions our world is in.

Jung Journal: Culture & Psyche for "The World Is Drawn on Wheels"

Michigan State Universities Libraries—Short Edition for "Caddle," "Quarter Moon," and "On the Sea There Is No Shade"

Oyster River Pages for "A Girl Reading in the Library" under the title, "Girl and Buffalo"

Sangum for "History of Texas"

The Raven's Perch for "Impossible Invasion from the North Pole"

Unleash Lit for "Reading" and "John the Revelator in the Garage"

ACKNOWLEDGMENTS

The Lost Notebooks of the Painter's Wife

Anthropoid for "Mukat and Temayawit" and "Self Portrait" under the title, "The Primal First"

Caliban online #24, July 2016, for several sections of "The Lost Notebooks of the Painter's Wife" with the author notes: A piece of writing has other writing circling around it. Sometimes I recognize the after-images or under-images, and sometimes I don't. I finished a play, "Lloyd and Hallah," about a painter and his wife. Throughout the play, Hallah keeps notebooks of Lloyd's words about his art. After his death, Hallah gives them to an art dealer, who loses them. After I heard a reading of the play at Oklahoma City Theater's 2016 Native Festival of New Plays, the notebooks began to appear, or the ghosting of them in my imagination, as though they really existed, as though Hallah existed also, and was still working, this time including some of her own words. Sometimes the messiness of writing bothers me. You think you have a project finished, but it keeps going. Morphing. As though it was an act of its own.

Flying Ketchup, Dark Forest Issue, the 2020 Button Prize for "The Game Event," "National Register of Historical Places" and "The Painter's Wife—I could face the bare pages."

Imagined Theatres: Writing for a Theoretical Stage, a Collection of Conceptual Events, edited by Daniel Sack, Taylor & Francis / Routledge, Oxfordshire, UK, 2017, for the first section of "The Painter's Wife" and "An Explanation Tale," with a Gloss about how the play continued after the writing was finished. How some of the missing pages came back to Hallah in dreams.
The Gloss—
The Lost Notebooks of the Painter's Wife
I finished writing a play, Lloyd and Hallah, about a painter and his wife. The play deals with appropriation, kleptomania and tuberculosis. After the painter's death, his wife takes the notebooks she has kept for years

to the art dealer, in hopes of continuing the sale of his work. The notebooks contain the painter's words about his style and method. The art dealer misplaces the notebooks.

The problem—this happens after the play ended. The play knew it was over, but the writing continued. Not writing that was another act in the play, but independent of it.

In *The Lost Notebooks of the Painter's Wife*, the missing pages come back to her in various dreams, arriving as a comet, and the painter as an elk in an animal transformation, and words that have no one to answer them. Often, the pages of the notebooks appear to the painter's wife out of order. In surreal images. Stripped of logical connection. But in the undergrowth, a reasoning shrouded in the dispersion.

What would I do with the after-play? Was it an Act II?—I thought at first. No, it was its own entity. Traveling out there in space.

Re: the notebooks. A syllogism marked the aftermath—
A tree is alive.
The pages of the notebooks are made from a tree.
Therefore the notebooks are alive.

The setting is Winnemucca, Nevada. Surrounded by mountains, desert and the evaporated Winnemucca Lake, where some of the oldest petroglyphs are found. Above her at night, the dark sky where comets, meteors [falling stars], and satellites cross.

Theater is not an object like a book. It happens across the stage in a passing-comet scenario. Made of dirt, dust, and the ice of conflict. And then it is gone, leaving the viewers with impressions. What I had left in the lost notebooks was the tail, so to speak, trailing from the comet, blown back by solar wind.

I see the painter's wife wearing the square covers of a notebook, neck to ankles, the way I've seen young men on television jump from cliffs in their flying suits [wing suits] to sail on the wind.

See the Elephant, *Metaphysical Circus*, for portions of the manuscript under the titles, "Footnote [2]," "Footnote [fragment of] [8]," "Footnote [34]," "Footnote [42]," "Footnote [55]," "Hallah," under the title, "The Lost Books of the Painter's Wife"

Tending the Fire, Native Voices & Portraits, Christopher Felver, Photographer, University of New Mexico Press, 2017, for "The Storyteller"

Westview, Southwestern Oklahoma State University, for "Part One: The Man Who Loves Dreamsicles" and "Part Two: The Erring Need of Narrative" under the title, "Writing the Idea"

Acknowledgment to a Fritz Scholder exhibit, National Museum of the American Indian, Washington, D.C. Somewhere in museum travel, I wanted to see writing framed as visual art is framed. I wanted to see, in part, poetics constricted into story. Acknowledgment to that persistent desire to make *storyature* of the disciplines.

Acknowledgment also to America's Interstates where I found ideas driving I-80 across Nevada. Elko—Winnemucca—Reno. For the General Theory of Identity and the incompatibility of constant and relative forces.

The Lost Notebooks of the Painter's Wife travels against the grain of its own fabric to deflect a childhood accident. It is what is left after the wind blows through.

On that trip, I drove from Kansas to Nevada. 820 miles—Shawnee Mission, Kansas to Rifle, Colorado, the first day. 765 miles—Rifle to Lake Winnemucca / Reno the second day.

There is light in summer. Fifteen hours of it. Driving west, another hour of light is there to meet you. It is all there is to do on the way from Kansas to Winnemucca.

The mountains in Colorado rise to the sky. They are obstructions to the road. A work of construction to get through—the four lanes of I-70 east / west travel, the railroad track, and the Colorado River crowd into narrow gorges between the mountains.

As a small child, in WWII, I went with my mother from Kansas to San Francisco to visit her sister. The train would have passed on the track beside the Colorado River. In Reno, I fell from the stopped train, and had the side of my nose sewn back onto my face.

After dark, in the rain, along I-70 in Colorado, I saw a Walmart in a small mountain town off I-70. I turned off the highway and slept in my car on the back edge of the parking lot.

The next morning at Starbucks, I asked what town it was. *Rifle*, she said. Because it was Sunday morning, I heard, *Rightful*.

Back on I-70, I saw the name of the town, and knew she had said, *Rifle*.

The sky was charcoal. There was more storm to drive through.

Parachute—another town farther west.

At the end of the mountains, there was rough road. Then mesa country. Beware of falling rock. Deer crossing frequently. Gusty winds. Curving road. Speed limit 75 miles. The highway passed through tunnels for east / west traffic, and there beside the larger tunnels, was a small tunnel-opening for the small train my mother and I rode.